P9-DMS-969

343016

DISCARD

CENTRAL-ADULT

Central

FORM AND TEXTURE
a photographic portfolio

FORM AND TEXTURE
a photographic portfolio

Ned Harris

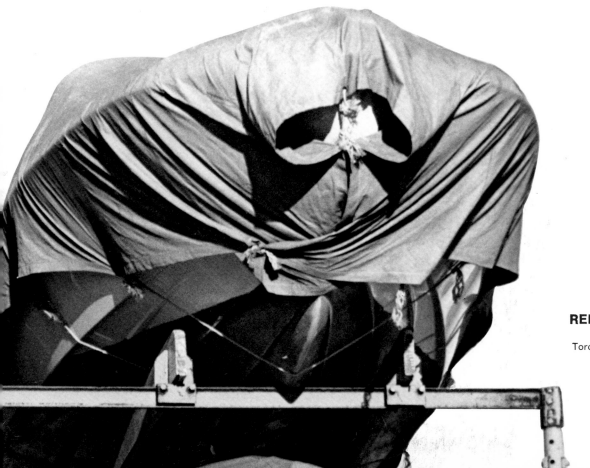

VNR

**VAN NOSTRAND
REINHOLD COMPANY**

New York   Cincinnati
Toronto   London   Melbourne

343016

To Sarah,
Mitchell, Felicia, Clifford, and Bryan

DESIGNED BY NED HARRIS

Van Nostrand Reinhold Company Regional Offices:
New York Cincinnati Chicago Millbrae Dallas

Van Nostrand Reinhold Company International Offices:
London   Toronto   Melbourne

Copyright (c) 1974 by Litton Educational Publishing, Inc.
Library of Congress Catalog Card Number 73-16706
ISBN 0-442-23157-1 (cloth)
ISBN 0-442-23159-8 (ppr.)

All rights reserved. No part of this work covered by the copyright hereon
may be reproduced or used in any form or by any means —
graphic, electronic, or mechanical, including photocopying,
recording, taping, or information storage and retrieval systems —
without written permission of the publisher.
Manufactured in the United States of America.

Published by Van Nostrand Reinhold Company
A Division of Litton Educational Publishing, Inc.
450 West 33rd Street, New York, N.Y. 10001
16 15 14 13 12 11 10 9 8 7 6 5 4 3 2 1

Library of Congress Cataloging in Publication Data

Harris, Ned. form and texture.

1. Visual perception.

2. Composition (Art)

3. Texture (Art) I. Title.

N7430.5.H37 701'.8 73–16706
ISBN 0-442-23157-1 (cloth)
ISBN 0-442-23159-8 (ppr.)

CONTENTS:

INTRODUCTION

The forms and textures of today are as unique as the times we live in. To become aware of their existence is a means of seeing and understanding reality. The words *form* and *texture* appear in every discipline attempting to crystallize experience. They are included in the popular vocabulary of all the arts and are used in a variety of ways in everyday language. Looking for form is a drive towards simplification, unity, and order; while texture counterpoints the need for complexity and embellishment. These are broad definitions which have to be more specific in their relation to the visual arts. In the context of this book, form refers to the spatial and dimensional materials of the physical world — a place that is filled with things that can be felt and touched. Texture is seen as form's outer skin, making the two inseparable partners. They are treated as existing properties which merely have to be discovered. The tool employed is the camera, advancing to see texture; retreating to observe form. The camera is today's most effective investigative and research tool for the visual arts, with its potential for helping to build one's own reference file and its ability to record precisely the quality of the material being researched. In the past, schools, museums, and libraries were the main source of inspiration and information — but the present atmosphere encourages a personal sense of discovery that seeks inspiration outside established walls.

Historically, the medium an artist used was dictated by tradition and the technical limitations of the time in which he lived. A painter accepted prescribed technique and spent his lifetime perfecting one style. Those working in form were confined to using stone or wood, while the craftsman followed long traditions of working with metal, fiber, leather, or clay. One discipline remained isolated from the other, and the rules that were established took generations to evolve. This is in sharp contrast to the mood of today in which everything accumulates, mixes, and is disposed of at an ever-increasing rate. This proliferation has created new landscapes filled with unique relationships of forms and textures.

Added to the traditional tools available to the artist and craftsman is the galaxy of man-made materials. Every season seems to herald a new line of synthetics that contain every conceivable quality; smoothness-roughness, opacity-clarity, softness-hardness, wetness-dryness, lightness-heaviness, in endless combinations. The quality of a new material, or the fascination with its surface, can be enough to inspire the contemporary artist. Within the material lies the message. A painter is no longer expected to maintain the flatness of his picture plane. All these new materials suggest surface relief, while they encourage the craftsman, sculptor, and architect to interchange techniques in democratic fashion. The camera helps break down barriers between these disciplines.

The atmosphere of diversity and change has been the perfect culture for the ascendance of the camera. Initially, it was a limited tool of the scientifically oriented or the craftsman, who attempted to imitate other traditions of the period. It was an elitist device. In contrast, today it is universally accepted, and available to the expert and the novice for expressing countless points of view. While many use it for entertainment, there have always been dedicated people attempting to create a new language. Recently, photographers have emerged who are using the camera as a natural extension of their perceptions. It is their constant companion, alerting them to an unexpected moment, and serving as a connecting link to other mediums. Although, within the framework of this book, the photograph can be viewed as an inspirational source in itself, its main purpose is to appeal to all the visual arts. The close-up textural details are intended for those working on the flat picture plane or on surfaces, while the formal examples should appeal to those working in the three-dimensional area.

There are two main currents affecting the examples of form and texture presented here. The emphasis is on a growing awareness of the interrelationship of the natural world mixing and mutating into manufactured materials. It has always been the fashion to depict the natural world as idyllic, pure and poetic — protecting itself against technological monsters. Artists have usually followed separate paths, isolating the natural from the urban. In order to break down these barriers I have included unexpected manufactured objects found at natural sites, showing how they are transformed in their new environment. When I move into a completely industrial or urban area there is no obvious evidence of nature, but my intention is to reveal its presence by showing that inorganic material can have the sensuous, growing, changing qualities which we associate with the organic.

To stimulate an awareness of so many influences, I have used a technique familiar to the photographer. I have gone to sites that are commonplace, to emphasize the availability of everything. They are locations for exercises in seeing. Each chapter is introduced by an array of contact-size photos, all of equal importance and emphasis. The intention is to show the world normally scaled, to avoid the distortion of a telephoto or microphoto approach. In order to discover the hidden forms and textures, the areas of interest are enlarged and resequenced. There is no retouching or darkroom manipulation, since the aim is to depict things as they are found in their original state. With this in mind, all the material was photographed with available light.

On an archaeological dig, fragments at the excavation site are meaningless. They are given some connecting order at a later, calmer moment. Similarly, I have grouped my own fragments afterwards, according to the material they are made of. The method of isolating sites emphasizes the changes that occur to the same materials at diverse locations. Wood formed at the water's edge is distinctly different from wood formed inland or in an urban area. Tires discovered on a beach, in the woods, at a dump, on a moving vehicle have different meanings. There is a sense of dislocation when the functional becomes useless. A tire that ceases to help you get somewhere turns you in a new direction; it starts to take on individual characteristics instead of duplicating its assembly-line partners.

Observing the extreme transformations of all materials by tidal waters led me to search for similar phenomena at other sites. In the beginning chapters, I work at natural sites — the sea, the land, the river — with organic materials — water, sand, rocks, wood, and vegetation. Signs of civilization become evident in the appearance of rubber, metal, rope, plastic, and paper, which fuse and finally dissolve into their environment. The next site is an industrial landscape where man-made products are manufactured and assembled, followed by a chapter on their disposal at a suburban dump. If these are the sites of making, then breaking — the urban area is where things are used and abused. The concluding site is the city, which is like a magnet attracting all things made and discarded. There is no evidence of people at any of the preceding sites, since they would distract from the world of things. The industrial area was deliberately photographed on Sundays, so that the human form would not upstage all the others. The city streets were receptive to all material. It is almost impossible to avoid people in the city — and it seemed unnatural to exclude them. However, their faces, were too dominant, and I decided to avoid them. What happens when the human frame is seen as a conveyor or armature for all the previously discovered textures? As a figure moves or rests, is isolated or in various multiples, complex relationships take place. In conclusion, the medium of the human form, enclosed by synthetic textures, seems to embody all the other messages in this book.

THE SEA

The classic area for beginning a search is at the land's end. It's the traditional site for experiencing nature as the ultimate creator of forms and textures; beachcombing becomes an extension of the selectivity of one's vision. The ceaseless tides, like a sculptor, chisel the rocks, manipulate the sand, and assemble the remnants from the sea in endless relationships. It's the ideal location for adjusting your sights to the camera's lens—challenging your ability to move from wide-angle, total viewing to isolated, close-up detail. The rocky coastline is a testing ground for the contrasting scales of monumental boulders to hand-size rocks. The photograph reveals the relationship and repetition of similar phenomena in the most diversely sized things. The stillness of stone contrasts with the turbulence of the water. Here is a primary lesson in seeing the camera as a tool for stopping the action of water in order to understand its force and ability to transform the most resistant of materials. A change of focus occurs when unexpected man-made materials are discovered—newcomers in a very old neighborhood. The flotsam and jetsam adapt themselves to their changed environment, becoming remarkable impersonators of their new neighbors. These found objects are quickly lost at sea, but their momentary uniqueness can be recorded by the camera.

WATER POWER

The rhythm of a wave
is repeated on the surface of stone.

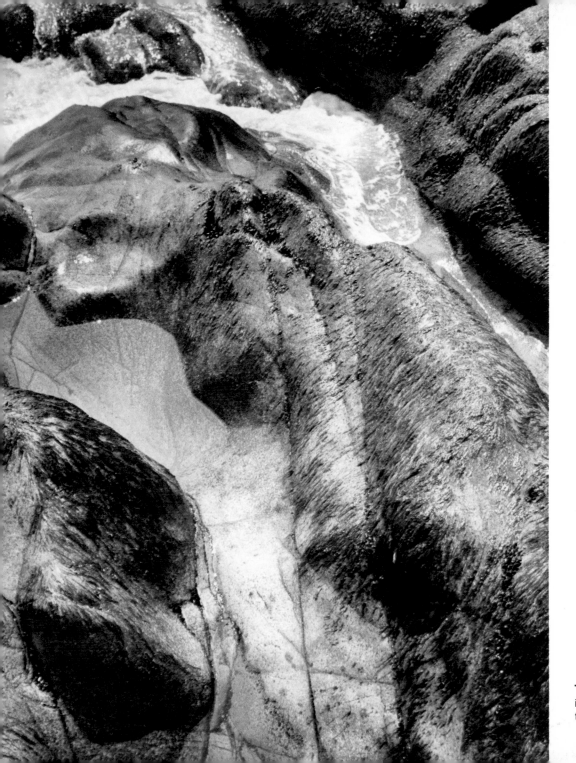

THE FORMING PROCESS
is revealed by stopping
the action of water.

A TIME STUDY

This Page:
The ebbing tide leaves momentary
forms in its wake.
Opposite Page:
Stone monuments that took
millennia to form.

SAND SCULPTURE

Situated beyond the tidal waters, the forms are
created by the erosion of the rainy season and the
hardening process of the sun.

ORGANIC ROCK

The accumulation of
primary life growing on rock
is a texturizing process.

NATURAL SELECTION
This Page:
An example of found sculpture
selected from a sea wall.
Opposite Page: Three views of the same rock
about actual size.

FLOATING ROCKS

Castaway plastic foam adapts to its
environment by imitating rock.

CAMOUFLAGE

A dislocated paperboard box acquires the characteristics of its rocky environment.

UNCOMMON OBJECTS are formed when the familiar is
exposed to the tides. These manufactured things
become one-of-a-kind objects when they're stripped
of their original function and appearance.
This Page: A rubber ball.
Opposite Page: Two plastic sandals.

UNEXPECTED FUSIONS occur when the natural and the unnatural share the same tidal pool.
This Page: A garland of snails on a beer can.
Opposite Page: A smooth glass bottle becomes texturized by barnacles.

TRANSFORMATIONS
A study in
perpetual change

This Page:
A changing fragment
of soft plastic.

Opposite Page:
Sunken inner tube — inflated.
One month later — deflated.

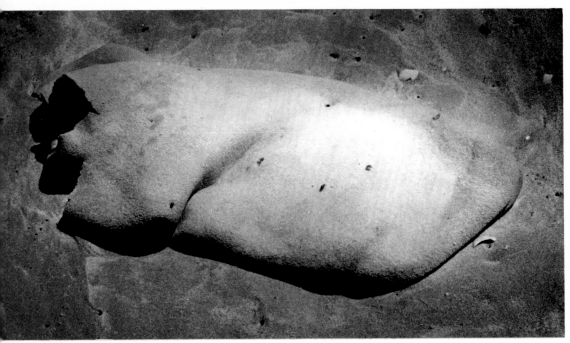

EMBEDMENT
A rubber arch punctured with a metal rod
and covered with ice and barnacles.

THE RIVER

At this site we see the same mixture of natural and man-made materials that appeared at the seashore. However, in adapting to a new environment, many changes take place. At the river's edge, pieces of wood are detached from their origins; fragments from old sinking barges and eroded abandoned piers become isolated objects on the shore, smoothed and polished by water and sand. Wood is a connecting link between shore and river — a place for expanding our interest in new materials. It is difficult to investigate the river without becoming aware of its use as a commercial avenue, where industry begins to dominate and overshadow the natural landscape. The boat leads appropriately into man-made materials; it is a floating laboratory containing a unique assortment of forms and textures. Once on board it's necessary to forget its original function, to re-orient our perception of its components. At sea, materials are accidentally mixed and fused; the seasons and the tides slowly change rocks and wood. On the river, the man-made is in its intended place. Metal, rope, canvas, rubber are all used for a specific purpose. Here the materials are given new meanings and functions by the new forms that they take in their continued usage.

FREEZING AND DRYING
Two conditions
that distinguish
the river from the sea.

ENCASED OBJECTS

A rubber tire and metal can
reflect the contrast in seasons.

WOODEN TOTEMS
This Page: Wood smoothed by sand.
Opposite Page: Wood eroded by water.

THE SHIPWRECK

This Page: Detail of rotted wooden side with metal bolt.
Opposite Page: Assortment of extracted bolts.

47

BOATYARD OBJECTS
Similar textures connect a metal rudder
with an anchor chain.

TUGBOAT TAPESTRY
Zooming in on the side of a tugboat
reveals rubber and fiber cushions.

WINTER STORAGE
Out of water and canvas covered—
the boat changes its personality.

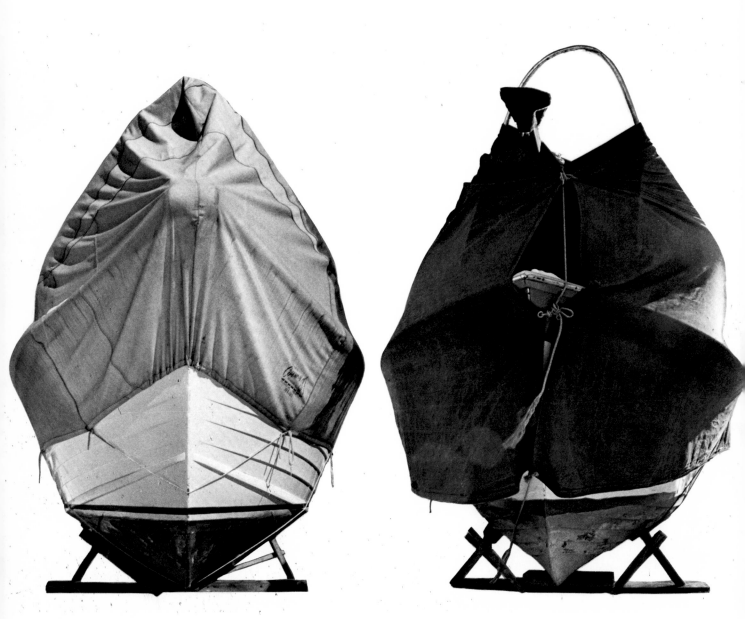

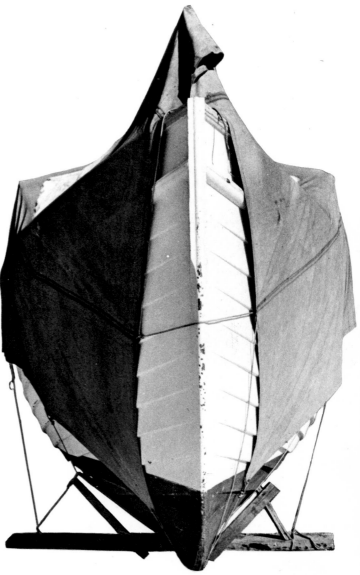

THE LAND

If stone crystallizes the meaning of the sea, then wood is its counterpart on land. Since even the camera finds it difficult to separate the forest from the trees, this area offers more of a challenge in isolating and simplifying the essential. The land is complex territory, since the abundance of material can be confusing and distracting. The forest is often depicted in impressionistic terms; light and shimmering foliage are used to evoke a romantic state. The objective of the camera in this environment, however, is not to paint a beautiful picture, or to assist in botanical research. Our concentration and intention here are focused on examples of materials that heighten our awareness of growth and change. The transformations at sea are measured in millennia; on land in seasons. In contrast to the inertness of rock, wood is an organic, active agent, sensuous in the way it overflows, fuses, and twists around all obstacles. Even after the tree dies, life flows from it through exotic fungus formations and the organisms that hasten the texturizing process. Man-made materials on land become additional elements in the interrelationship of all things, which results in unique combinations of forms.

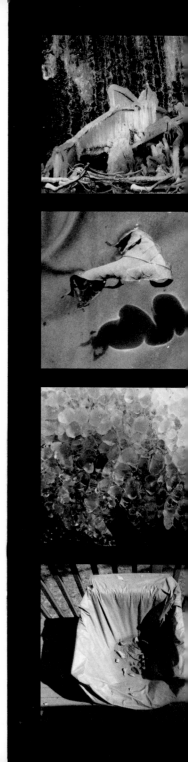

FROZEN LANDSCAPE
Branches form the armature
for ice sculpture.

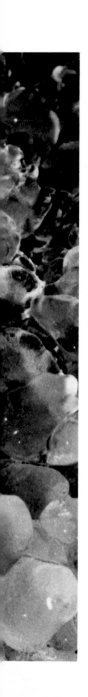

TWISTED FORM
Different stages of
distortion created by vines
fusing into tree trunks.

BARK PAINTING
Close-up detail
of two tree trunks.

THE CROSS-SECTION
Looking down at the
exposed insides of two tree stumps.

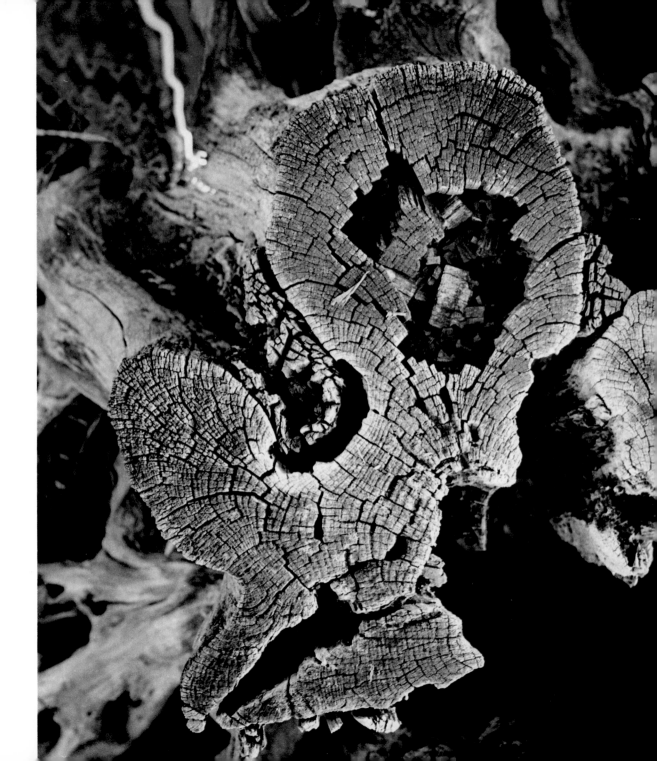

ORGANIC CHANGES

This Page:
A spider changes
the form of a leaf at a pond.

Opposite Page:
A growing fungus
and a dried one
pierced by a metal rod.

SPRING PLANTING
Worm's eye view of wrapped roots
being maneuvered for planting.

THE GROWING PROCESS

This Page:

A tree found enveloping
a metal townhouse fence.

Opposite Page (left):
Detail of flowing bark
around a brass finial.

Opposite Page (right):
The same detail two
years later.

FLOATING LEAVES
A covered chair is a receptacle for
water and two dried leaves.

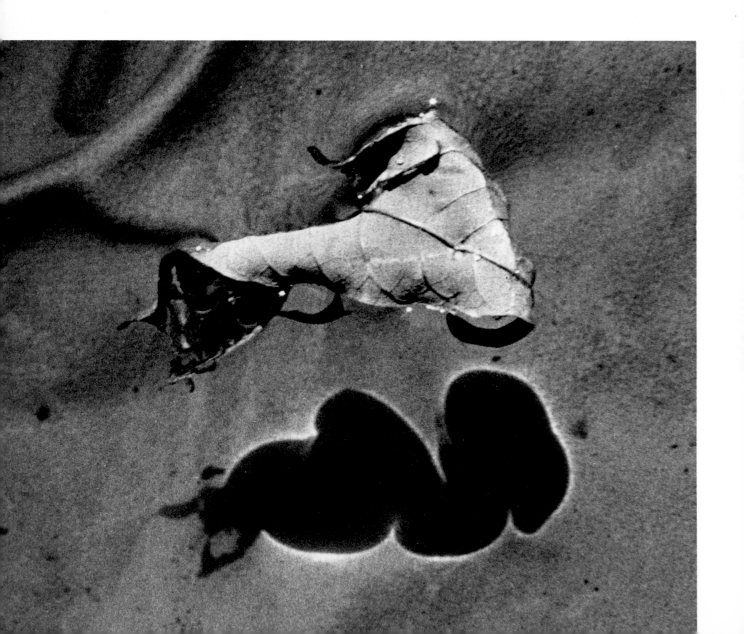

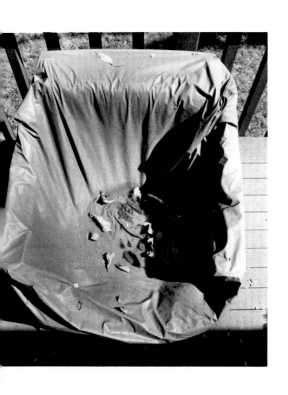

THE INDUSTRIAL SITE

Water is the only connecting link between this man-made landscape and the previous natural sites. The area is first seen from the river, where large geometric shapes are littering the shoreline. They contrast with other discarded, one-of-a-kind found objects, small enough to blend into their environment. Cement conduits are manufactured here, an assembly line of huge primary forms. They are a galaxy of stored and stacked shapes that can be walked through and around, an accidental architectural playground. Among these concrete assemblages are some individual pieces that, in their isolation, take on a totem-like monumental quality. In addition to the finished product, all the materials necessary to the manufacturing process itself can be seen — metal molds, cement mixers, hardware, industrial furniture, and bent, twisted wire used for armatures. Smaller in scale, these by-products are photographed at close range, revealing the texturizing effects of grit, grease, and dried cement. This site is challenging because it encourages a double vision — of both large geometric forms and small textural detail, similar to that previously seen on the surfaces of rocks and trees.

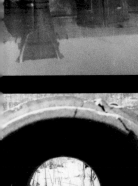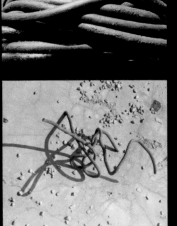

TIDAL GEOMETRY
Forms change when the
incoming tide is seen through cement cylinders
resting at the river's edge.

PRIMARY FORMS
This Page:
A cast cement form and its metal mold.
Opposite Page:
A geometric landscape of cement castings.

THE COVERED OBJECT
The same metal mold as on page 78
with the addition of a canvas cloth.

A metal claw viewed
from four angles.

BENT WIRE
used as armatures
for cement cylinders.

METAL ASSEMBLAGE

Accidental combinations of metal equipment.
Approximate height of the form
on this page — twelve feet.

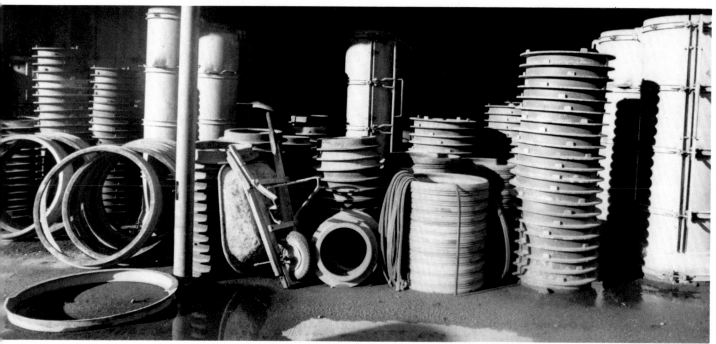

A FAMILIAR FORM
changed by the elements,
and its conversion
to a functional object.

SEEING DETAIL
This Page:
A fragment of paper on a truck.
Opposite Page:
The metal hinge on a door.

THE ANTHROPOMORPHIC OBJECT
The face of a cement mixer and a close-up of
its outer skin — dried cement on metal.

MIXED MEDIA
A combination of steel and rubber
covered with grease.

THE WASTELAND

At the industrial site we concentrated on things being structured, duplicated, and assembled, while here, all is discarded and destroyed. The brutal landscape of our abandoned, once cherished belongings, now overwhelming and plaguing everything in sight, is a familiar contemporary scene, one of upheaval and displacement of commonplace possessions — a change that makes the familiar grotesque. It records the ecological crisis and strengthens the naturalist's polemic. In looking for source material with the camera, the wasteland is not intended as editorial territory. However, it is a place that evokes an apocalyptic mood, making it more difficult to be cool and objective. The most dramatic and dominant element, even in its dormant state, is the automobile. When new, it is today's icon of status and necessity. In a wrecked state, having lost all its class and style, every car has equal importance. There is only a twisted, bent, crushed, and compacted mountain of material that beckons the searching scavenger, the artist, and the photographer. Shattered glass, plastic, fabric, rubber, and metal — this last the most prevalent material — is all that remains. Rock is the most prevalent material at sea, wood on land, metal in the wasteland.

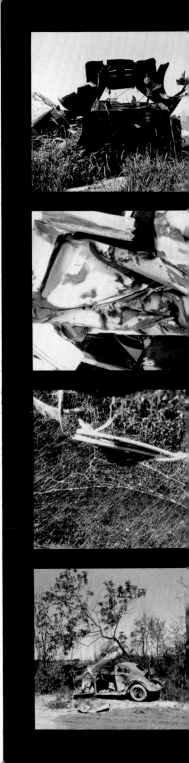

CRUSHED CARGO
Last year's model becomes
one compacted mountain of steel.

THE ORGANIC ENGINE
Looking under the hood, a spider's web-work
replaces the motor.

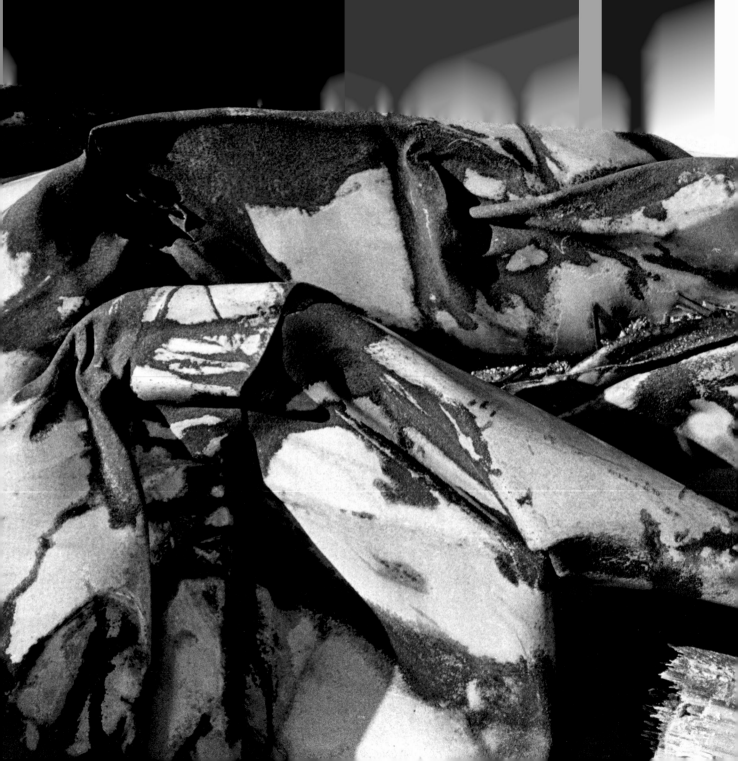

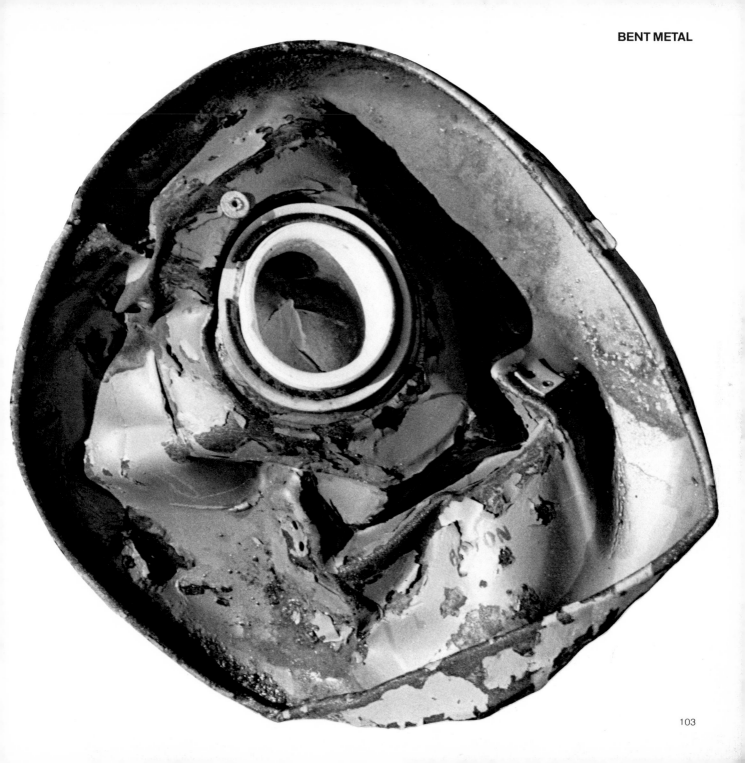

RUSTED METAL
Hood surface of an abandoned car
reflects its natural locale.

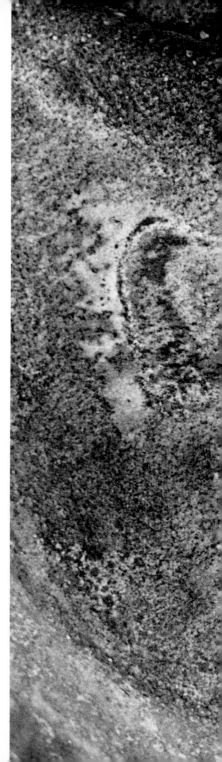

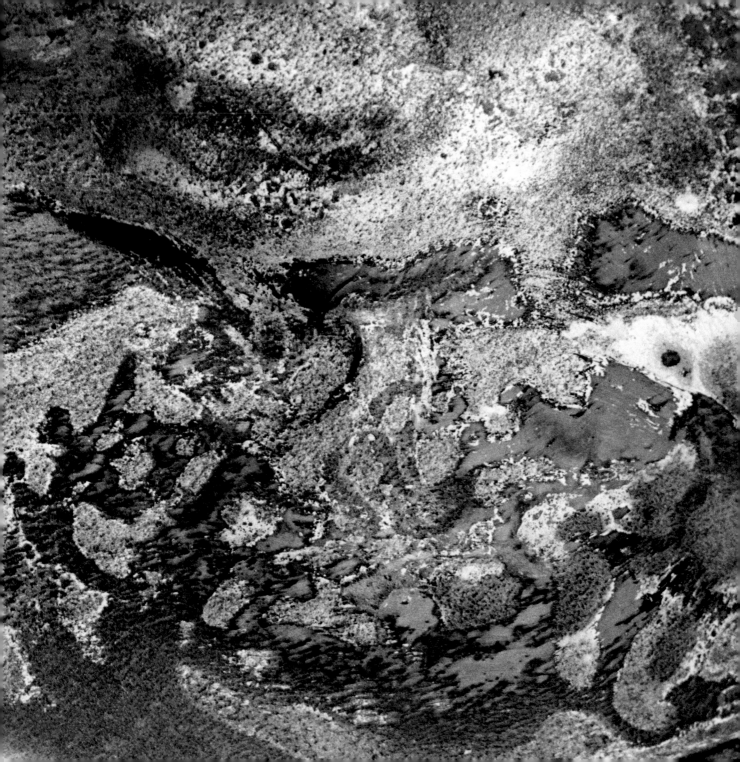

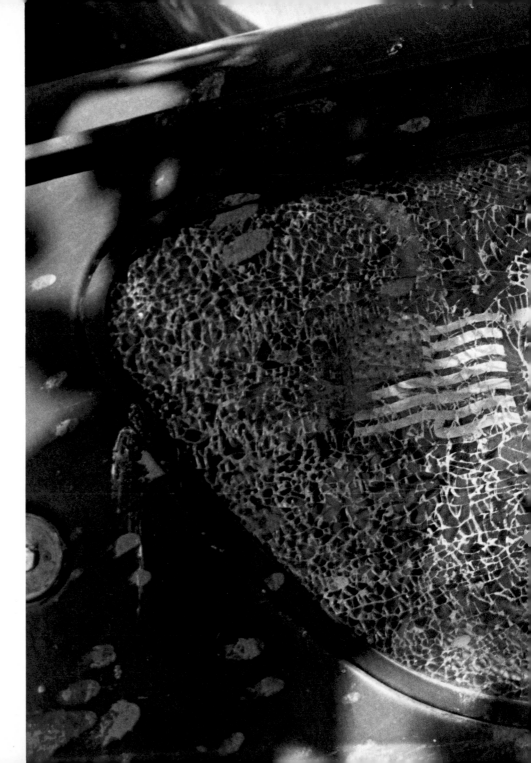

SHATTERED GLASS
A broken window is a mosaic
of glass and decals.

A STEEL FRAGMENT
Remnant of a
wheel's inner drum.

THE CITY

The natural, manufactured, and discarded objects that have been shown serve as an introduction to the urban scene, which is like a collage of the unexpected. At other locations, I have emphasized the fusing of the natural and the man-made. In the city, however, people become the natural element, assimilating with the material world they have created. This is the marketplace where all the products of our technology affect everyone and change the way the world has traditionally looked. Everything we see and purchase seems to be wrapped, tied, packaged, and sealed, ready to be shipped or sold. When people are seen in the same context, they seem to acquire the qualities of a marketable package—they become part of the plethora of merchandise. The recurrent theme of finding inspiration in the commonplace and the available is given added meaning in the city. People mix with paper, wood, fabric, fiber, steel, glass, and plastics. The constant movement and change requires the use of all the visual lessons learned at the previous sites. In this dynamic setting, seeing photographically becomes an intuitive, reflex action. The camera is the ultimate tool for communicating this sense of mixed media and the transposition of people and products.

BENT GLASS
Reflections in distorted glass

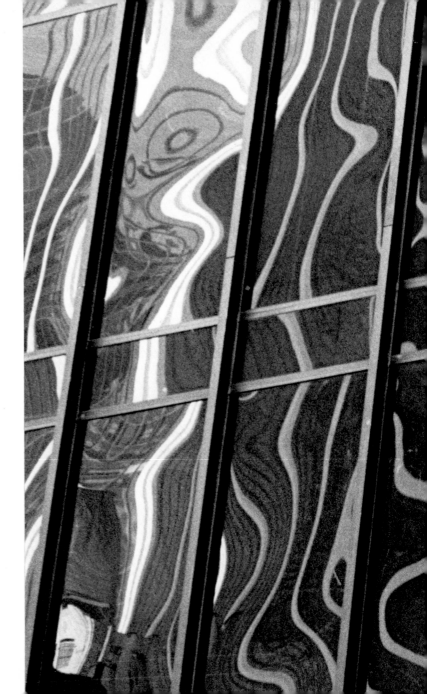

TORN PAPER
A close-up of the shredded pages
of a collapsing telephone book.

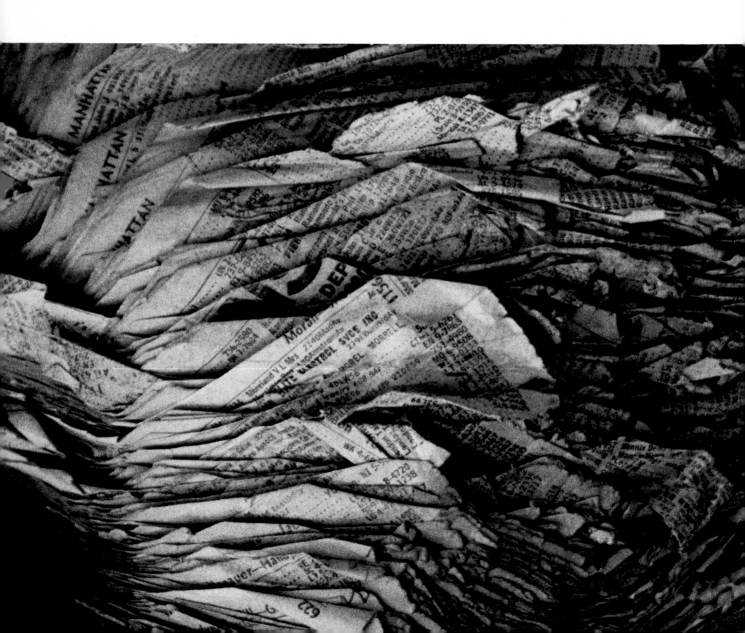

PAPER SCULPTURE
This Page:
A pedestrian with
a self-made rain hat.

Opposite Page:
Peeling wallpaper on an
abandoned building.

AGED WOOD

This Page:
The remnants of a
demolished building.

Opposite Page:
An inner-city door.

METAL SCULPTURE

This Page:
The tattooed car becomes a
personalized collage.

Opposite Page:
A totem-like wastebasket
burned in the line of duty.

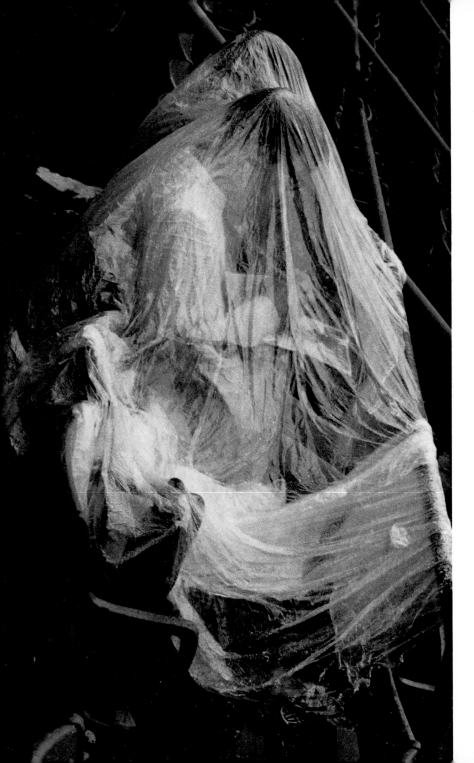

TRANSPARENT PACKAGES
Protection from the elements
transforms the familiar.
This page:
Plastic-covered people.
Opposite page:
A building under construction.

A FOOD HANGING

A woven tapestry
of packaged foods.

FIBERS
An interplay of fur, hair, and people.

A commonplace mop becomes an unusual object when used as a tool for repairing a city street.

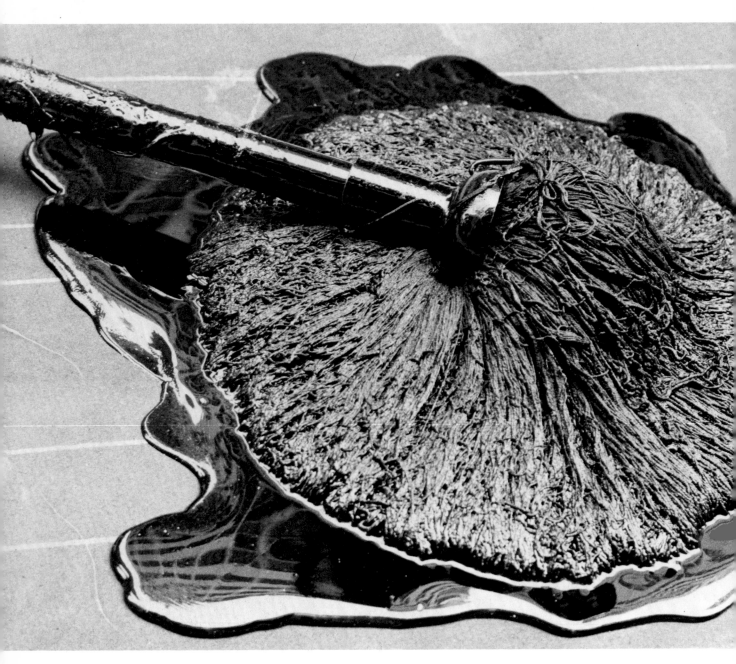

MIXED MEDIA
A combination of wrapped-up objects.

THE FLEXIBLE OBJECT
Street furniture by
Con Edison joins
a man bending and walking.

THE BACK (SIDEWALK SITTING)
Seated figures are a study in mixed forms and textures.

 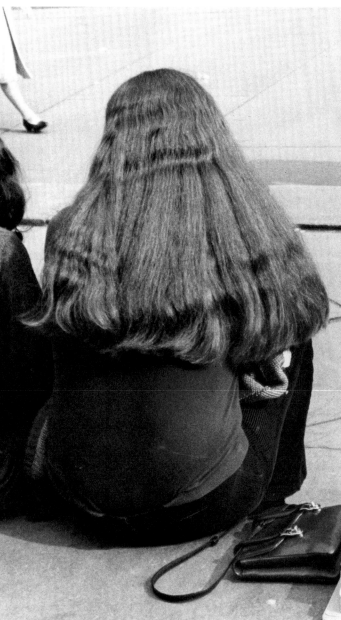

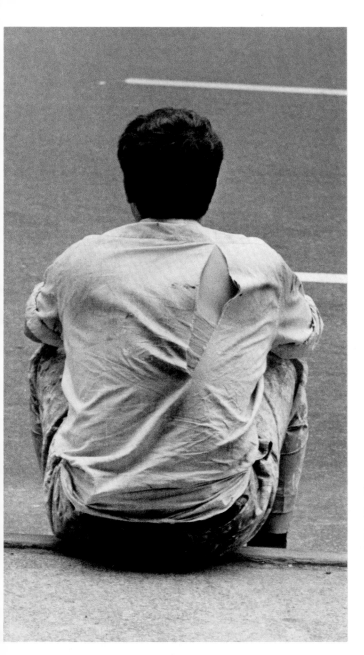

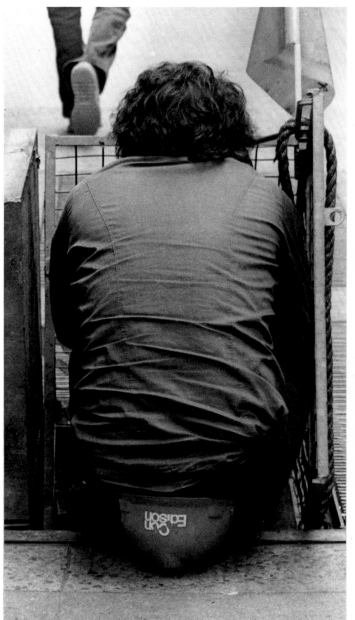

THE TRANSPORTERS
The human figure combines with the material
it pushes, pulls, and carries.

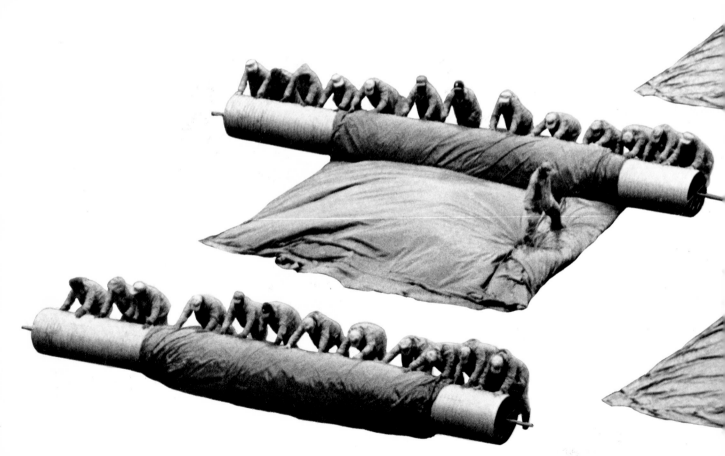

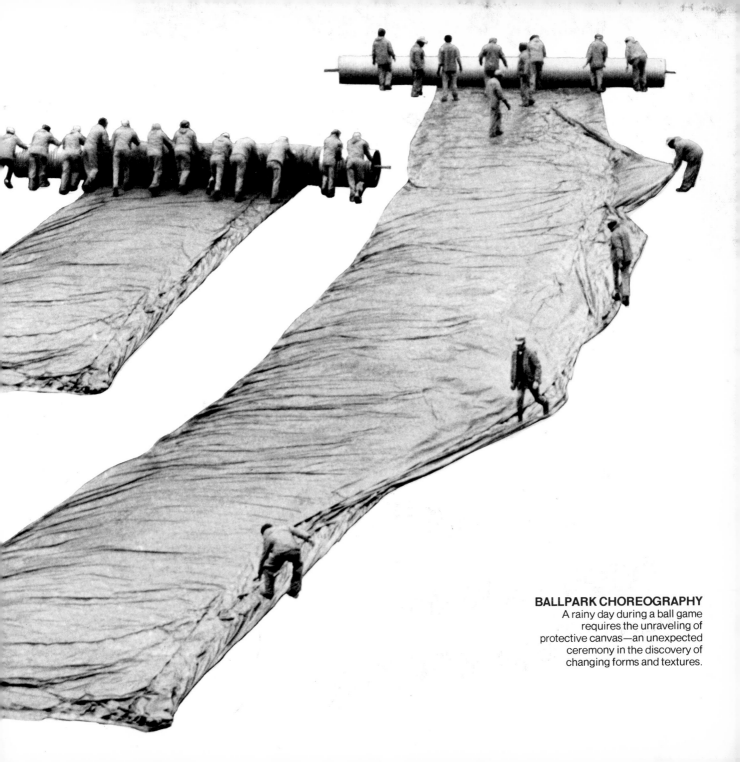

BALLPARK CHOREOGRAPHY
A rainy day during a ball game
requires the unraveling of
protective canvas—an unexpected
ceremony in the discovery of
changing forms and textures.

A FREE FORM found in a city park.